Written by L. J. Onzo

Illustrations by Noah Higgins

ISBN: 978-1-66785-127-3

Annie was the best artist in the whole world!

Mommy had all of Annie's artwork proudly

displayed on the refrigerator so

that proved it!

Annie loved to draw people and flowers and animals and trees, and bugs on trees.

Every picture was very different, and every picture was very beautiful.

Annie was going to visit her best friend, Emma, in the hospital. Emma had to have her tonsils removed, which meant she could have all the ice cream she could eat! Annie loved ice cream almost as much as she loved drawing. Chocolate chip was her favorite. All morning she worked on a special picture for Emma. She drew a great big bowl of chocolate-chip ice cream, smothered in gummy bears and rainbow sprinkles and marshmallow fluff, and right on top sat Annie and Emma. They were getting down to the serious business of ice cream eating.

As they drove to the hospital, Mommy reminded Annie of their agreement. "Now, Annie, remember to use your 'inside voice', and no running in the hallways, okay?"

"Okay." Annie stared out the window. "And then we are getting the ICE CREAM!" She sang this at the top of her lungs, and heard laughter from the front seat.

Annie imagined herself reclining on a giant banana split, covered in ice creamy goodness, and munching on a maraschino cherry the size of her face.

She thought about this for a moment and smiled.

While Annie was picturing her next masterpiece, Mommy pulled into the hospital parking lot. They parked the car and walked to the main entrance. The big glass doors opened with a SWOOSH and a blast of cool air.

Annie walked briskly to the elevator, careful not to bend her artwork. Up to the third floor they went. BING! The doors opened, and Annie was skipping down the hallway before she could help herself.

"Annie," called her mother, "remember our agreement."

"Okay." Annie slowed down to a speed-walk,

her mother in hot pursuit.

When they reached Emma's room, Annie was disappointed to see that she was asleep. "Can we wake her up?" Annie asked this in a loud whisper, hoping to do just that.

"No, Annie," said the nurse already there. "Nap time is very important. It helps us to stay strong."

Annie scrunched up her face. This was the same line Mommy gave her at home. Suddenly though, she didn't feel so bad about taking her afternoon nap. Maybe Mommy was on to something.

"I have an idea," said Mommy. "Why don't we take a walk about and have a look around. Then we can get some ice cream, and bring it back here. Emma should be awake by then."

Annie was all for that. She loved taking walks with Mommy because Mommy always made everything an adventure. And the best adventures always ended with ice cream.

Annie carefully placed her picture on Emma's bed stand, knowing that it would be the first thing that Emma saw when she woke up. Resisting a strong urge to give her sleeping friend the tiniest nudge, Annie took her mother's hand, and they were on their way.

Down the corridor they went. There were so many things that Annie had never seen before. "Mommy, what's that?" she asked, pointing to a little boy in a wheelchair.

"No pointing, Annie," said Mommy. "It isn't polite."

Annie dropped her hand at once.

"That's a wheelchair. It helps people get around when they can't use their legs."

"Why can't he use his legs, Mommy?" Annie waved to the boy, and smiled broadly.

"I don't know, Sweetie. Some people are born that way, and some people may get in an accident or get sick."

The little boy waved back at Annie and smiled in return.

"On the outside he is in a wheelchair," said Mommy, "And on the inside he's just like you and me."

Annie thought about this for a moment and smiled. "Okay, Mommy."

"Would you like to see the babies?" Mommy asked, already knowing the answer. "YIPPEEE," cried Annie, and catching herself whispered, "Yippee."

As they walked back to the elevator, Annie spied a grandpa walking towards them. "Mommy, what's that?" she asked, careful not to point.

"That's a walker, Annie," said Mommy. "Some people need help to walk so they use a walker."

"Why don't cha use a wheelchair instead?" Annie asked, looking up at the grandpa.

"Oh, aren't you just precious," he chuckled. "Well, you see, doll, my legs work okay, but they get tired easily, so I use this here walker to help them out."

"On the outside he uses a walker," said Mommy, smiling at the grandpa, "And on the inside he's just like you and me."

Annie thought about this for a moment and smiled. "Okay, Mommy."

They waved goodbye to the grandpa and were on their way.

Back on the elevator they went. "What floor do you need?" asked the young woman already there. "Two, please," replied Mommy.

The woman pressed the button and, catching Annie's stare, smiled and introduced herself. "My name is Claire."

"I'M ANNIE." Annie forgot her inside voice and her manners as she stared at Claire's hand. It didn't look like any hand she had ever seen before. "Mommy, what's that?"

Mommy sighed and looked sheepishly at Claire, who smiled warmly and spoke first.

"This is called a 'prosthetic'". It's an artificial hand. Some people, like me, are born without an arm or a leg, and some might lose them in an accident. This prosthetic helps me to do almost anything you can do."

"Can you draw with it? And eat ice cream?" Annie asked, scratching the tip of her nose. "I sure can," said Claire, bending down to Annie's eye level. "Chocolate-chip is my favorite."

"Me, too!" Annie got a closer look and grew quiet. "Does it hurt?"

"No, honey. It doesn't hurt at all." Nose to nose, Claire and Annie smiled at each other.

"On the outside Claire wears a prosthetic," said Mommy, smiling gratefully at the other woman, "And on the inside she's just like you and me."

Annie thought about this for a moment and smiled. "Okay, Mommy." BING! The elevator doors opened, and they waved goodbye.

Down the hall they went. Annie was so excited she could hardly contain herself. She could hear the distant cries before she could even see where they came from.

"Here, Annie." Mommy lifted her up in front of three large windows.

Annie's eyes widened when she saw all the tiny babies in pastel bundles, their little beds in three neat rows.

"They all look the same," Annie said, somewhat disappointed.

"I know," Mommy agreed, "but when they get bigger, they will all look very different. Some might be very tall, and others might be very short."

"Miss Julie comes to class every Friday and teaches us how to garden," piped Annie. "She's a grown-up, but I'm almost as big as her."

"I know, Sweetie. Miss Julie is a little person," Mommy explained. "On the outside Miss Julie is smaller than most, and on the inside she's just like you and me."

Annie thought about this for a moment and smiled. "Okay, Mommy."

"Some babies may grow up to be very thin, and some may grow up to be very heavy," Mommy continued, as Annie smushed her face against the nursery window.

"Some may have to wear braces to straighten their teeth. Some may have to wear glasses to help them see better, and some may not be able to see at all.

Some may need to wear a hearing aid to help them hear better, and some may not be able to hear at all."

"We are all born looking pretty much the same, but as we grow up, we develop our own unique looks and our own special talents. All of these babies will grow up to look very different on the outside," stated Mommy, "And on the inside – "

"They'll be just like you and me," said Annie.

"That's right, Sweetheart," Mommy said, giving Annie a great big hug. "Just like you and me. Now let's go get that ice cream."

Annie thought about this for a moment and smiled. "Okay, Mommy."